Creating Comics

Robin Johnson

CRABTREE
PUBLISHING COMPANY
WWW.CRABTREEBOOKS.COM

Title-Specific Learning Objectives:

Readers will:

- Understand what comics are.
- Describe the process used to make comics.
- Explain how both words and pictures can be used to tell a story.

High-frequency words (grade one) can, have, help, make, put, that, they, who, with	Academic vocabulary artist, character, computer, dialogue, plot, setting

Before, During, and After Reading Prompts:

Activate Prior Knowledge and Make Predictions:

Bring examples of familiar comic strips and comic books to class and show them to the children. Ask how many of them read comics or comic books, and name their favorites. Then ask how the stories told through comics are different than stories in other books.

Hold up *Creating Comics*. Ask a volunteer to explain what the word "create" means. Then have children guess the steps they think might go into making a comic. Record their answers on the board. Tell them they will look at their guesses again when they are done reading the book.

During Reading:

After reading page 5, call children's attention to the comic strip with the dogs. Ask:

- What information would be missing if you only had the words?
- What information would be missing if you only had the pictures?

After Reading:

Have children revisit their guesses about the steps that go into making a comic. What was missing? Which steps were out of order? Create a new list that shows all the steps in the right order.

Author: Robin Johnson

Series Development: Reagan Miller

Editors: Bonnie Dobkin and Janine Deschenes

Proofreader: Melissa Boyce

STEAM Notes for Educators: Bonnie Dobkin

Guided Reading Leveling: Publishing Solutions Group

Cover, Interior Design, and Prepress: Samara Parent

Photo research: Robin Johnson and Samara Parent

Production coordinator: Katherine Berti

Photographs:

Alamy: Les Breault: p. 5 (b); Marka: p. 7 (t); Photo 12: p. 7 (b); Art Directors & TRIP: p. 8-9; Newscom: p. 16, thelittlegreyartist: p. 17 (bl); Greg Balfour Evans: p. 20

iStock: 2thirdsphoto: p. 4; Mediaphotos: p. 17 (t); portishead1: p. 17 (br), p. 18 (l)

Shutterstock: Sunshine Seeds: title page; Olga Popova: p. 6 (tl, bl); Wantanddon: p. 6 (br); Oldrich: p. 6 (br); Oksana Klymenko_But: p. 10; Catwalker: p. 12; Yackers1: p. 14, p. 21 (b); Savusia: p. 18 (r); ramlen salleh: p. 21 (t)

Wikimedia: public domain: p. 9 (tr)

All other photographs by Shutterstock

Library and Archives Canada Cataloguing in Publication

Title: Creating comics / Robin Johnson.
Names: Johnson, Robin (Robin R.), author.
Description: Series statement: Full STEAM ahead! | Includes index.
Identifiers: Canadiana (print) 2020016578X |
Canadiana (ebook) 20200165798 |
ISBN 9780778771906 (hardcover) |
ISBN 9780778772682 (softcover) |
ISBN 9781427124616 (HTML)
Subjects: LCSH: Comic books, strips, etc—Authorship—Juvenile literature. | LCSH: Comic books, strips, etc—Technique—Juvenile literature. | LCSH: Comic books, strips, etc—Juvenile literature.
Classification: LCC PN6710 .J64 2020 | DDC j741.5/1—dc23

Library of Congress Cataloging-in-Publication Data

Names: Johnson, Robin (Robin R.) author.
Title: Creating comics / Robin Johnson.
Description: New York : Crabtree Publishing Company, 2020. | Series: Full steam ahead! | Includes index.
Identifiers: LCCN 2019058738 (print) | LCCN 2019058739 (ebook) |
ISBN 9780778771906 (hardcover) |
ISBN 9780778772682 (paperback) | ISBN 9781427124616 (ebook)
Subjects: LCSH: Comic books, strips, etc.--Authorship--Juvenile literature. | Comic books, strips, etc.--Technique--Juvenile literature. | CYAC: Cartoons and comics--Authorship--Juvenile literature..
Classification: LCC PN6710 .J64 2020 (print) | LCC PN6710 (ebook) | DDC 741.5/1--dc23
LC record available at https://lccn.loc.gov/2019058738
LC ebook record available at https://lccn.loc.gov/2019058739

Printed in the U.S.A./032020/CG20200127

Table of Contents

Crabtree Publishing Company
www.crabtreebooks.com   1-800-387-7650
Copyright © **2020 CRABTREE PUBLISHING COMPANY**. All rights reserved. No part of this publication may be reproduced, stored in a retrieval system or be transmitted in any form or by any means, electronic, mechanical, photocopying, recording, or otherwise, without the prior written permission of Crabtree Publishing Company. In Canada: We acknowledge the financial support of the Government of Canada through the Book Publishing Industry Development Program (BPIDP) for our publishing activities.

Published in Canada
Crabtree Publishing
616 Welland Ave.
St. Catharines, Ontario
L2M 5V6

Published in the United States
Crabtree Publishing
PMB 59051
350 Fifth Avenue, 59th Floor
New York, New York 10118

Published in the United Kingdom
Crabtree Publishing
Maritime House
Basin Road North, Hove
BN41 1WR

Published in Australia
Crabtree Publishing
Unit 3 – 5 Currumbin Court
Capalaba
QLD 4157

What Are Comics?

A comic is a series of drawings that tells a story. A comic can tell any kind of story. Some comics tell funny stories. Others tell adventure stories.

Most comics use both words and pictures to tell a story.

Some comics are very short. They are called comic strips. You usually find them in newspapers.

Some comics tell longer stories. They are made into comic books that have many pages.

Telling Stories

Artists have been telling stories in comics for more than 100 years. Like all stories, comics have colorful **characters** and **settings**. They have interesting **plots**.

Superheroes have been featured in comics since the 1930s. They are characters with special powers.

Dennis the Menace is a comic strip that began in 1951. What do you think is happening in this picture?

The setting of this *Peanuts* comic is a baseball game in the summer. Setting is the time and place of a story.

Words and Pictures

A comic strip is made up of boxes called panels. Each panel has a drawing that shows a piece of the story. Panels also have words and **captions** that help tell the story.

Speech bubbles show what characters are saying.

Some panels show a scene. A scene tells where the story is happening.

Some panels have close-ups of a character's face. A close-up shows how a character is feeling.

A thought bubble tells what a character is thinking. It is usually shaped like a cloud.

A caption like this helps explain what is happening.

Some panels have sound effects. A sound effect is a word that describes a noise.

Panels in a Row

Comic artists put panels together to tell a story. Most comic strips are square panels lined up in rows.

This comic artist has put panels together to make a comic strip.

Comic books use panels too. They may be different sizes and shapes. The panels fill many pages.

Most comic books have dozens of panels. Many are over 20 pages long.

Getting Started

Every comic strip starts with an idea. It might be a brave superhero who saves the world. It could be a lazy cat who loves lasagna. Then a comic artist or a comic team gets to work creating the comic.

An artist came up with the idea for Garfield the cat in 1976. He is still making people laugh!

Artists may make **sketches** of their ideas as they work.

Writers and artists often work together on comic book ideas.

Planning the Comic

Writers and artists must plan their story before drawing pictures. They begin with a **script**. A script describes the characters, setting, and plot. It also includes what the characters will say.

A script shows all the events and dialogue in a story. Dialogue is what the characters say.

Next, writers and artists use a layout to plan what will go in each panel. A layout is a plan for how a comic will look.

Artists and writers often work together on layouts.

This layout shows a plan for a story about a girl and her family.

Drawing the Pictures

Next, a comic artist draws pictures that go with the script. The artist uses a pencil and paper or a computer to draw rough sketches. Then the artist goes over the pencil lines in black ink.

Artists use pencils or computers for sketches so they can make changes easily.

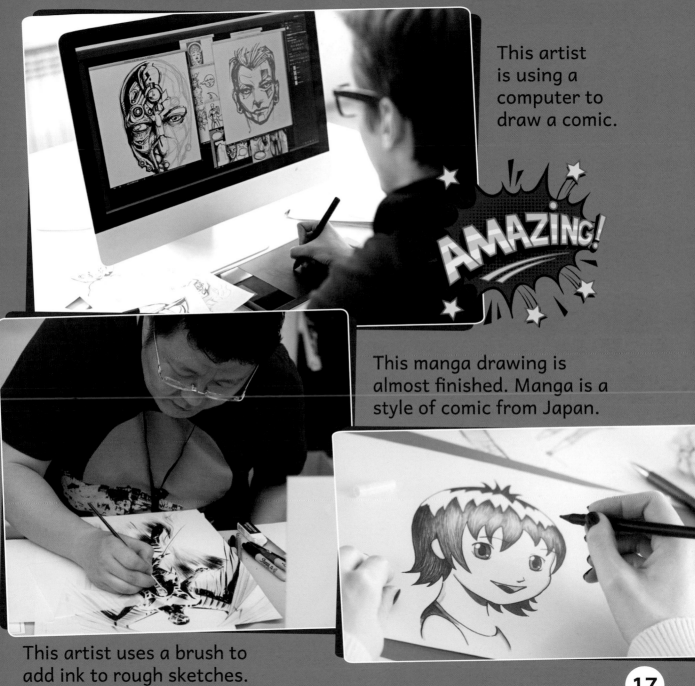

This artist is using a computer to draw a comic.

AMAZING!

This manga drawing is almost finished. Manga is a style of comic from Japan.

This artist uses a brush to add ink to rough sketches.

Final Steps

Artists may add color to their drawings. Color can make a comic seem funny, or scary, or exciting. Then the artist adds captions and other words that help tell the story. Finally, an **editor** carefully checks the comic for mistakes.

Artists use pens, paints, or computers to add color to their work.

Bright colors can show excited or happy feelings. Dark colors can show sad feelings. How does this colorful comic make you feel?

How does color change the look of this comic character?

The words in speech bubbles are usually the last things added to a comic.

19

Read All About It!

After comics are created, they are printed. You will see comic strips in newspapers and magazines. You can find comic books in stores. Comics are also shared online.

You can read comics just about anywhere!

This boy is visiting a comic book store.

People can buy comics at meetings called **conventions**. They can also see artists creating comics there.

Words to Know

captions [KAP-shuh ns] noun Words that describe what is happening in a picture

characters [KAR-ik-ters] noun People in a story

conventions [kuhn-VEN-shuhns] noun Meetings of people who have common interests

editor [ED-i-ter] noun A person whose job it is to correct and revise a story

plots [plots] noun The main stories of books, comics, plays, movies, and other works

script [skript] noun The written text of a story

setting [SET-ting] noun The time and place of a story

sketches [skech-es] noun Rough drawings that show a plan for what a picture will look like

A noun is a person, place, or thing.
A verb is an action word that tells you what someone or something does.
An adjective is a word that tells you what something is like.

Index

About the Author

Robin Johnson is a freelance author and editor who has written more than 80 children's books. When she isn't working, Robin builds castles in the sky with her engineer husband and their two best creations—sons Jeremy and Drew.

To explore and learn more, enter the code at the Crabtree Plus website below.

www.crabtreeplus.com/fullsteamahead

Your code is:
fsa20

STEAM Notes for Educators

Full STEAM Ahead is a literacy series that helps readers build vocabulary, fluency, and comprehension while learning about big ideas in STEAM subjects. *Creating Comics* helps readers understand how information is provided through both images and text. The STEAM activity below helps readers extend the ideas in the book to build their skills in both art and language arts.

Creating a Comic

Children will be able to:
- Develop ideas for a comic strip.
- Create a layout for their comic strip.
- Use words and pictures to tell a story.

Materials
- Making a Comic Strip Handout
- Script Template
- Comic Strip Worksheet (2 per child)
- One pencil and pen per child
- Colored pencils or thin, felt-tip markers

Guiding Prompts
After reading *Creating Comics*, ask children:
- What are the different parts of a comic?
- Why are both words and pictures important in a comic?

Activity Prompts
Tell children that they will now have a chance to create their own three-panel comic strip. Distribute the Making a Comic Strip Handout. Read the steps aloud.

Remind children that their first step is to come up with a story idea. The idea must include characters, setting, and a plot. (You may wish to give them the option of creating a strip using characters they are already familiar with.) Once they have their idea, tell them to write their script using the Script Template. Remind children that, like any story, their comic strip should have a beginning, a middle, and an end.

When they are done with their script, have them create a rough layout of what their comic might look like using the Comic Strip Worksheet. Encourage them to use rough shapes and stick figures and remind them to leave enough space for speech bubbles. Tell them they may have to change their script if their plan doesn't work.

When they are ready, children should make final copies of the strip on the second worksheet. This time, the drawing should be as detailed as they can make it. If they wish, they can add ink lines and color, just like a real comic artist would.

Extensions
- Display the comic strips around your classroom. Have children do a gallery walk to read what their classmates created.

To view and download the worksheet, visit **www.crabtreebooks.com/resources/printables** or **www.crabtreeplus.com/fullsteamahead** and enter the code **fsa20**.